Dot-to-Dots, Puzzles, and Games

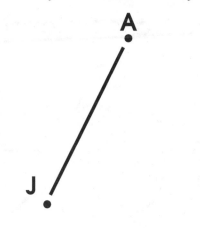

This book belongs to

_____

FS109018 Dot-to-Dots, Puzzles, and Games

Hungry Little Critter

Connect the dots from **a** to **f**. Color.

FS109018 Dot-to-Dots, Puzzles, and Games

Name _____

Find the Helmet

Help Katie find her helmet.

3
reproducible

FS109018 Dot-to-Dots, Puzzles, and Games

Name _____

Watch Out for My Web

Connect the dots from **1** to **10**. Color.

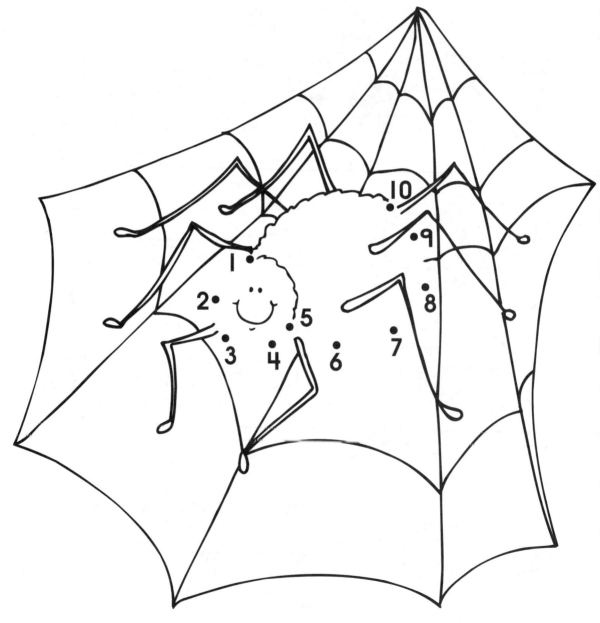

4
reproducible

FS109018 Dot-to-Dots, Puzzles, and Games

Let's Go!

Find the word in each row. Color the boxes that show the word.

a	b	o	a	t	o

t	r	a	i	n	n	e

a	n	p	l	a	n	e

c	e	c	a	r	r

Name_____

Swimming Bird

Connect the dots from **a** to **k**. Color.

FS109018 Dot-to-Dots, Puzzles, and Games

Name _____

Animal King

Connect the dots from **1** to **10**. Color.

FS109018 Dot-to-Dots, Puzzles, and Games

Name _____

A Colorful Flyer

Use the code to color the picture.

1 = yellow   **2** = orange   **3** = green   **4** = blue

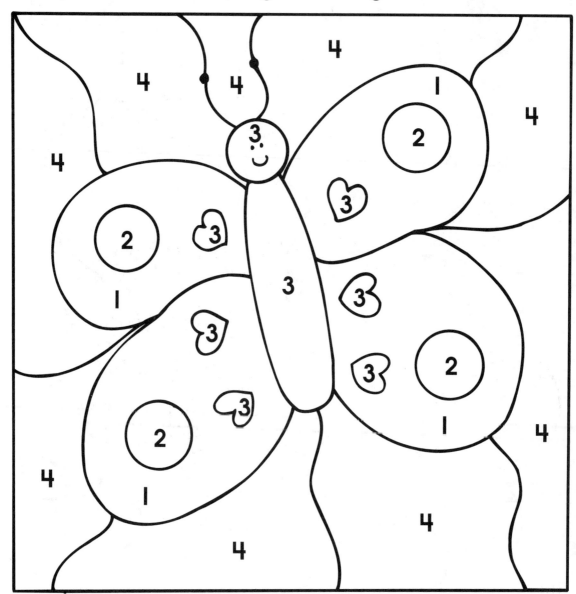

FS109018 Dot-to-Dots, Puzzles, and Games

Name _____

Fly Away!

Connect the dots from **1** to **10**. Color.

FS109018 Dot-to-Dots, Puzzles, and Games

Swamp Home

Help the alligator find its way home.

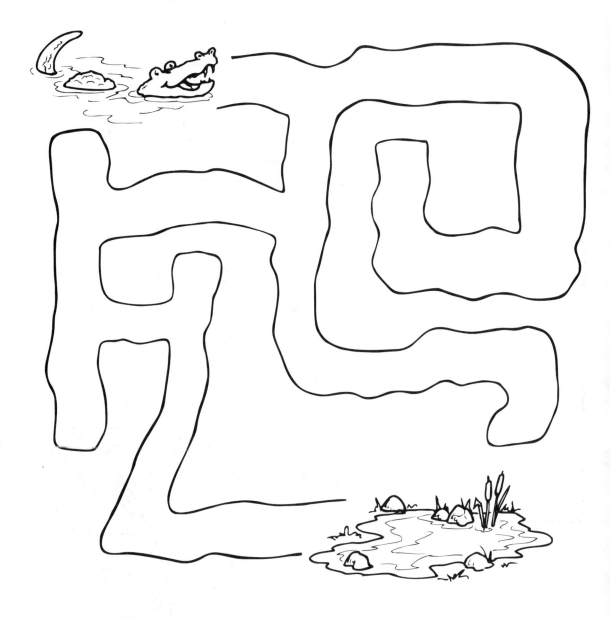

Name _____

Triangle Hunt

Find and color each triangle.

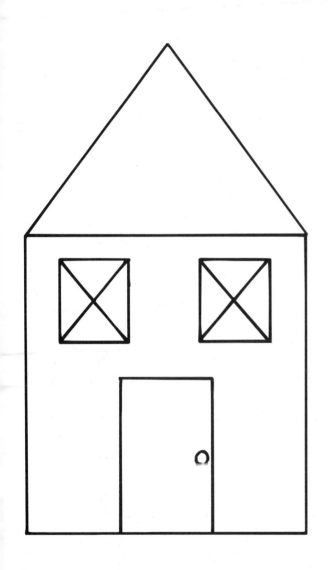

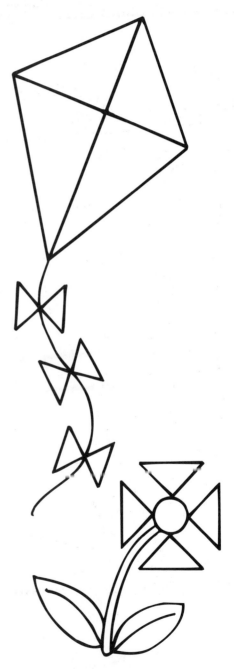

11
reproducible

Name _____

Shoot for the Stars!

Connect the dots from **A** to **G**. Color.

Name _____

Farm Animal Fun

Find the word in each row.
Color the boxes that show the word.

a	l	a	m	b	e

c	o	c	o	w	o

h	o	r	s	e	e

p	g	i	p	i	g

FS109018 Dot-to-Dots, Puzzles, and Games

Name _____

Ocean Mammal

Connect the dots from **A** to **L**. Color.

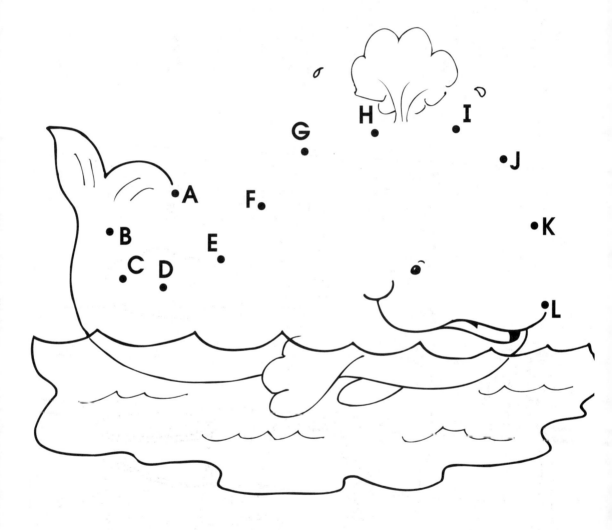

Name _____

At the Beach

Connect the dots from **1** to **10**. Color.

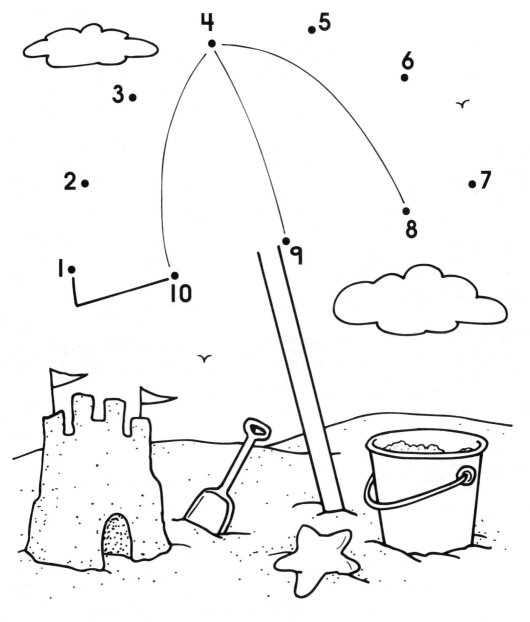

FS109018 Dot-to-Dots, Puzzles, and Games

Perfect Pets

Color the one that comes next in each row.

Name _____

Flying High

Connect the dots from **I** to **10**. Color.

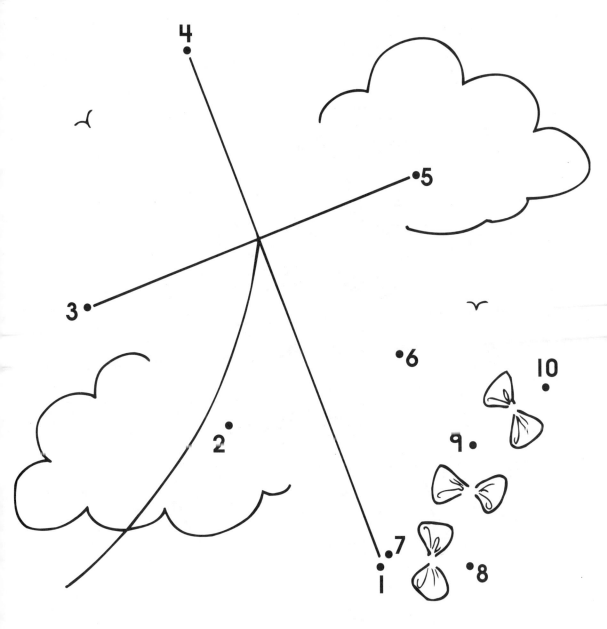

FS109018 Dot-to-Dots, Puzzles, and Games

Name _____

Let's Roll!

Connect the dots from **A** to **N**. Color.

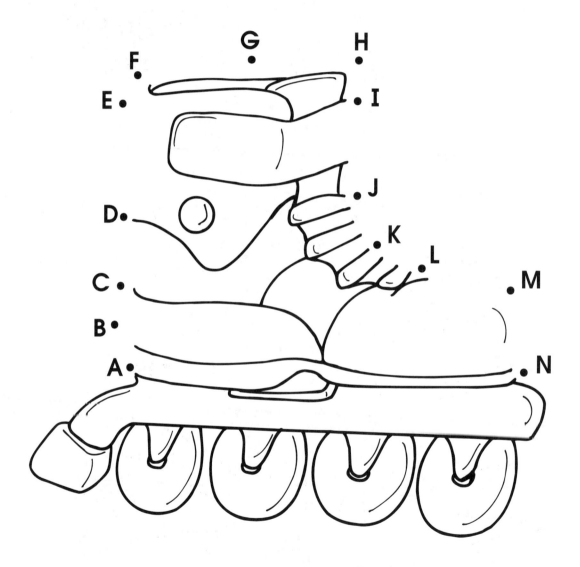

Name _____

Springtime Color

Connect the dots from **1** to **15**. Color.

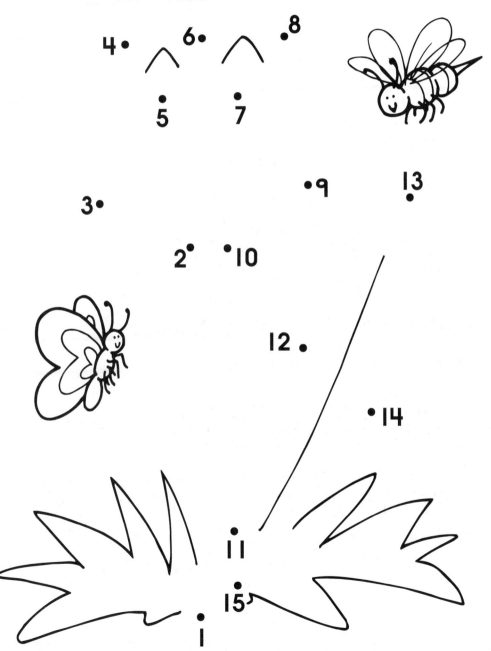

4• 6• •8
5   7

3•   •9   13

2• •10

12 •

•14

11

15

1

19 FS109018 Dot-to-Dots, Puzzles, and Games
reproducible

Name _____

Wonderful Water

Use the code to color the picture.

5 = blue   **6** = brown   **7** = red

8 = green   **9** = yellow

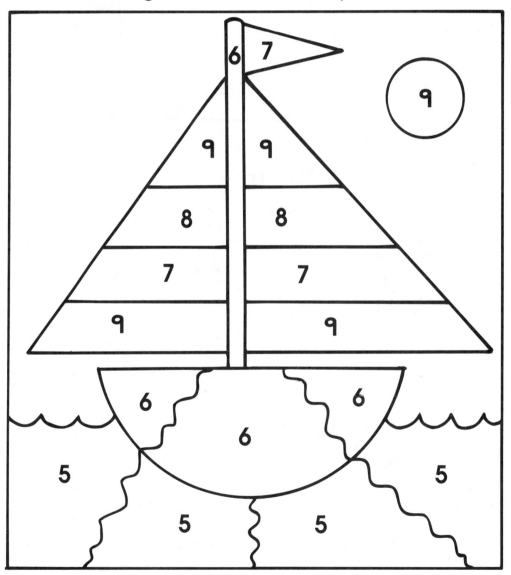

Name _____

Monkey Business!

Connect the dots from **a** to **n**. Color.

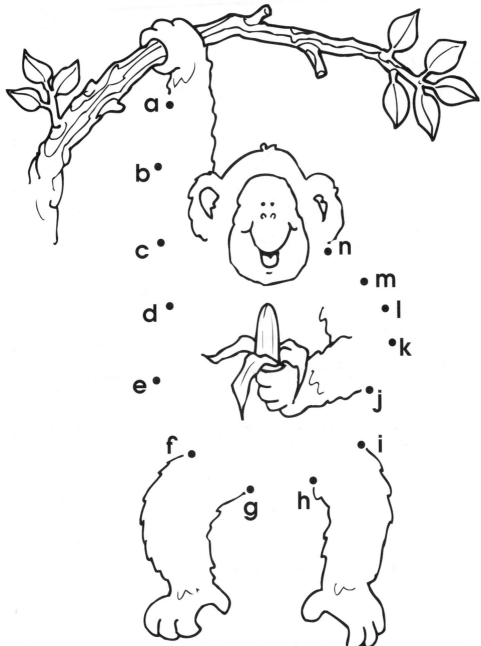

FS109018 Dot-to-Dots, Puzzles, and Games

Teddy Bear

Connect the dots from **1** to **15**. Color.

FS109018 Dot-to-Dots, Puzzles, and Games

Goodies for Grandma

Help Corey find her way to Grandma's house.

Name _____

Play Time

Connect the dots from 1 to 15. Color.

FS109018 Dot-to-Dots, Puzzles, and Games

School Stuff

Find and circle the words in the puzzle.

book

ruler

pencil

paper

p	e	n	c	i	l
a	b	o	o	k	p
p	c	p	e	n	m
e	f	r	u	l	e
r	u	l	e	r	n

Name _____

Cold Weather Fun

Connect the dots from **A** to **O**. Color.

FS109018 Dot-to-Dots, Puzzles, and Games

Name _____

Always at Home

Connect the dots from 1 to 15. Color.

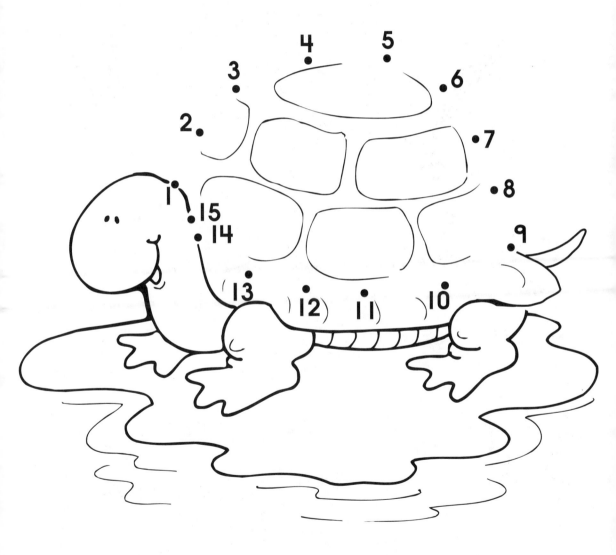

FS109018 Dot-to-Dots, Puzzles, and Games

Name _____

Hiding on the Beach

Find the numbers **1** to **6** and color them blue.
Then color the picture.

FS109018 Dot-to-Dots, Puzzles, and Games

Preparation

Remove the puzzle-card pages from the center of the book. Make a copy of these directions and then cut the cards apart. Then carefully cut each card into two puzzle pieces along the lines.

How to Play

These two-piece puzzle cards are self-correcting and can be used in a variety of ways. One or more children can play the following games:

Number Match: The puzzle pieces are mixed up and scattered faceup on a flat surface. A child chooses a puzzle piece that has a number on it and looks for the puzzle piece with the matching number of insects on it. Then the child puts the puzzle pieces together. If they fit, the child gets to keep them. If they don't fit, the child looks for another piece. One child can play this game alone. If there is more than one player, the children can take turns looking for matching pieces or looking for matches at the same time. Everybody wins when all the puzzles have been put together.

Number Memory: The puzzle pieces are mixed up and placed facedown in rows on a flat surface. A child turns over two puzzle pieces. If they match (if one is a number and the other is a picture of the matching number of insects), the child gets to keep the pieces and turn over two more pieces. If they don't match, the child turns the pieces back over and his or her turn is over. Then another child (or the same child if there is just one player) turns over two pieces to see if he or she can make a match. Play continues till all the matches are made. The winner is the child with the most pieces.

A

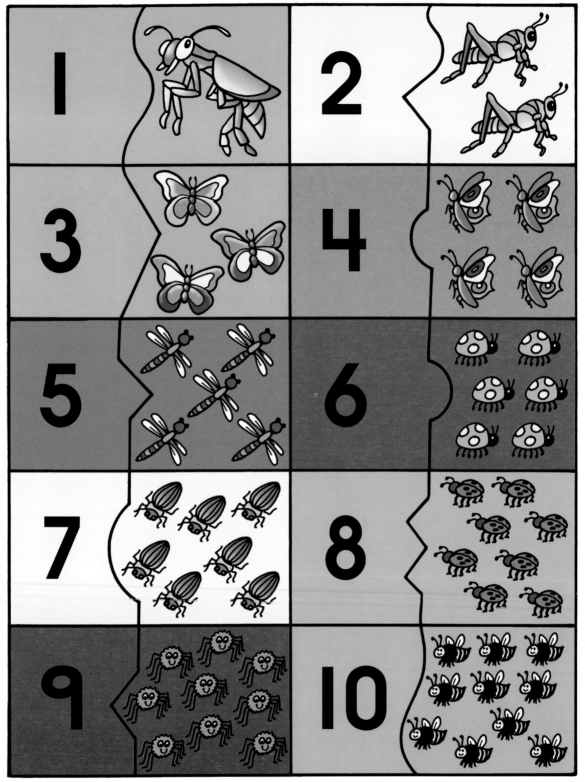

B

C

FS109018 Dot-to-Dots, Puzzles, and Games

D

Name _____

Big Roller

Connect the dots from **1** to **15**. Color.

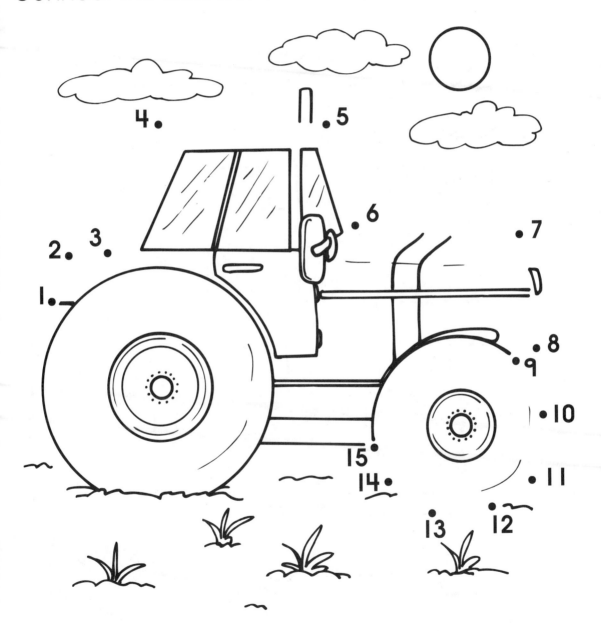

Name _____

Hungry Bunny

Help the bunny find the carrots.

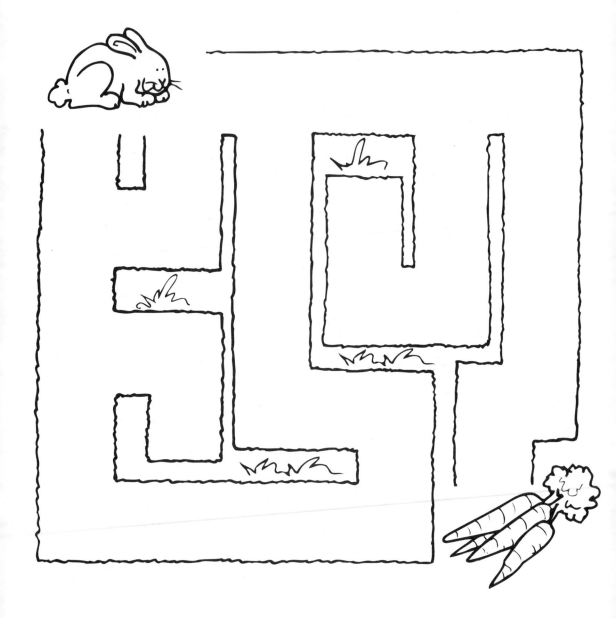

Name _____

Toy Time

Find and circle the words in the puzzle.

ball

doll

bat

bear

b	a	t	d
a	b	f	o
l	c	m	l
l	p	f	l
b	e	a	r

31
reproducible

Name _____

Horse Sense

Connect the dots from **a** to **n**. Color.

Name _____

Hop In!

Connect the dots from **A** to **Q**. Color.

FS109018 Dot-to-Dots, Puzzles, and Games

Clowning Around

Use the code to color the picture.

8 = red   9 = green

10 = purple   11 = orange

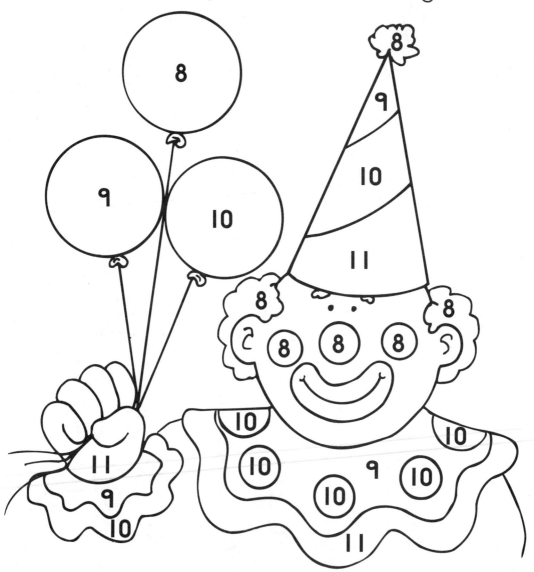

34
reproducible

FS109018 Dot-to-Dots, Puzzles, and Games

Name _____

Roundabout Fun

Find and color the circles.

35
reproducible

FS109018 Dot-to-Dots, Puzzles, and Games

Name _____

Blast Off!

Connect the dots from **A** to **T**. Color.

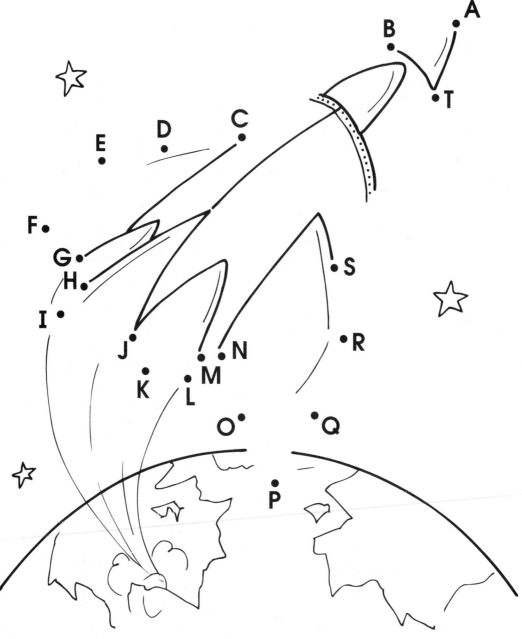

FS109018 Dot-to-Dots, Puzzles, and Games

Name _____

Floating in the Sky

Connect the dots from **1** to **20**. Color.

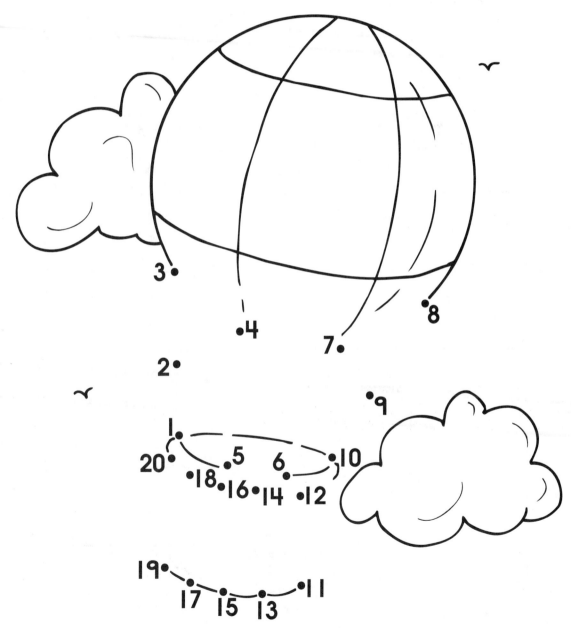

37
reproducible

Name _____

Where's the Picnic?

The ant is hungry. Help it find the picnic.

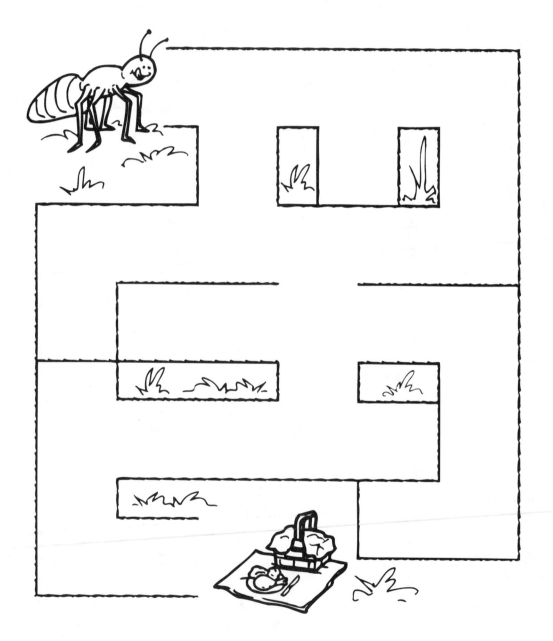

38
reproducible

FS109018 Dot-to-Dots, Puzzles, and Games

Fit for a King

Connect the dots from **I** to **20**. Color.

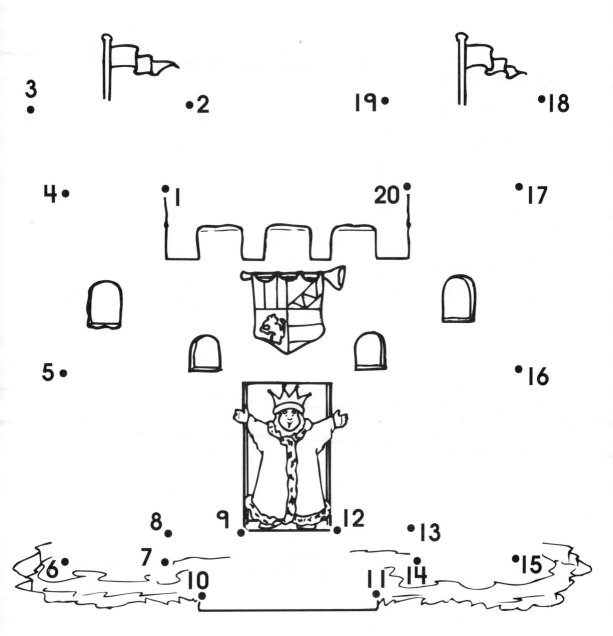

Flowers and Critters

Color the one that comes next in each row.

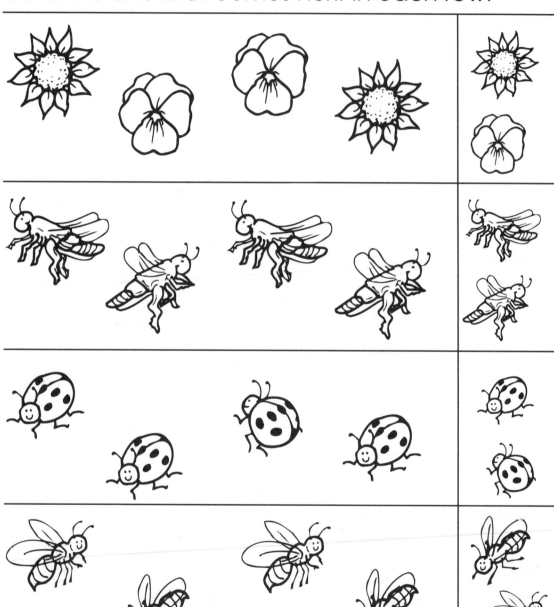

Name _____

Fishing Is Fun

Find 6 . Color them green.

What a Show!

Connect the dots from **a** to **t**. Color.

FS109018 Dot-to-Dots, Puzzles, and Games

Name _____

Super Fast

Connect the dots from **1** to **20**. Color.

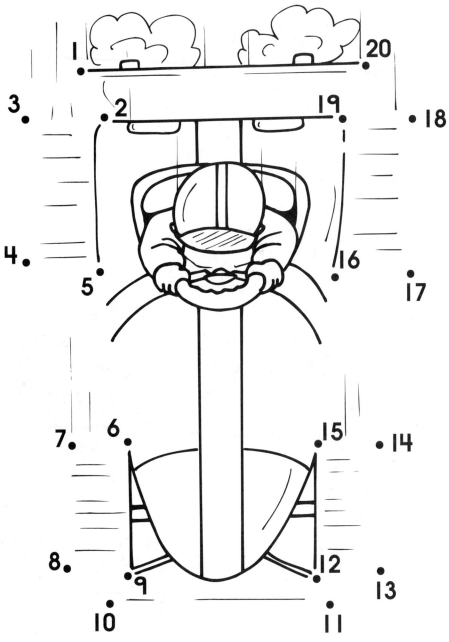

FS109018 Dot-to-Dots, Puzzles, and Games

Name _____

Up in the Sky

Write the words in the puzzle.

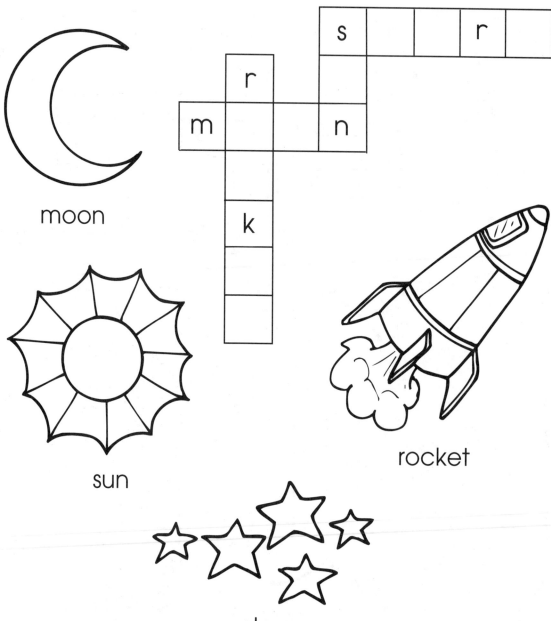

moon

sun

rocket

stars

FS109018 Dot-to-Dots, Puzzles, and Games

Name _____

Homework Time

Help Tommy find his homework.

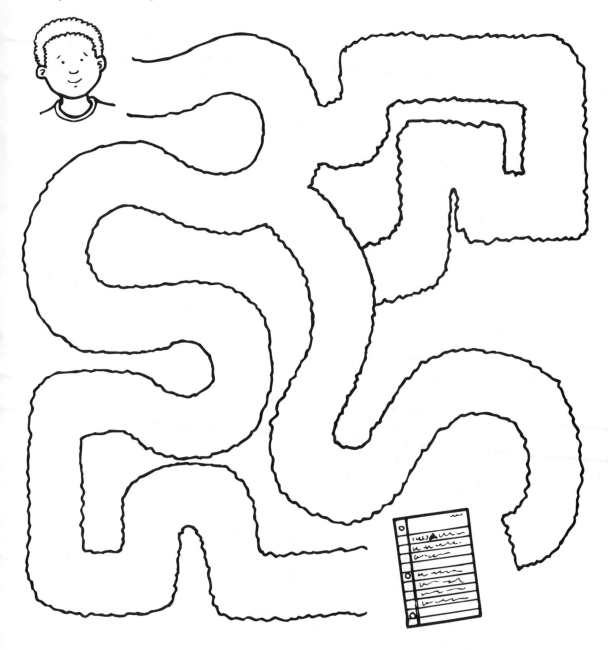

FS109018 Dot-to-Dots, Puzzles, and Games

Name _____

Long Ago

Connect the dots from **1** to **25**. Color.

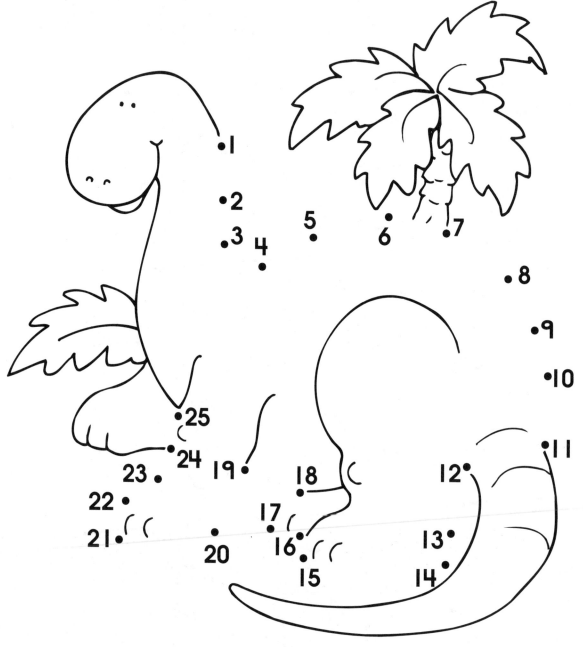

46
reproducible

Name _____

A Perfect Little Pocket

Connect the dots from **A** to **Z**. Color.

FS109018 Dot-to-Dots, Puzzles, and Games

Let's Go, Lindsay!

Help Lindsay find her soccer ball.

Name _____

Fresh Foods

Find and circle the words in the puzzle.

 apple

c	o	a	p	p	l	o
o	r	a	n	g	e	p
r	n	a	p	p	l	e
n	s	o	r	g	n	a
c	a	r	r	o	t	s
b	a	n	a	n	a	e

 banana

 carrots

 orange

peas

corn

FS109018 Dot-to-Dots, Puzzles, and Games

Name _____

Off to School

Connect the dots from **1** to **25**. Color.

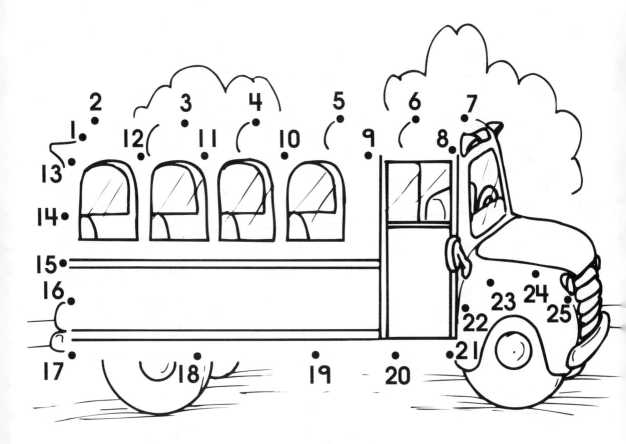

FS109018 Dot-to-Dots, Puzzles, and Games

Name _____

Wow! What Big Ears!

Connect the dots from **A** to **Z**. Color.

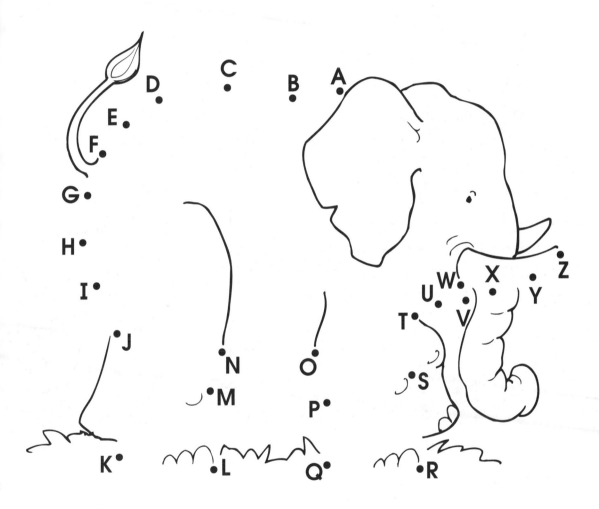

Happy Birthday, Casey!

Help Casey find her birthday present.

Sweet Treats

Find and circle the words in the puzzle.

candy

m	c	o	f	k	c	a
c	a	n	d	y	o	i
a	k	g	u	m	o	p
k	e	u	r	o	k	i
b	r	o	w	n	i	e
r	t	o	k	i	e	e

cookie

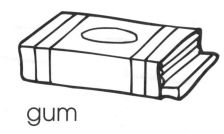

gum

brownie

cake

pie

Name ____________________

Little Critters

Write the words in the puzzle.

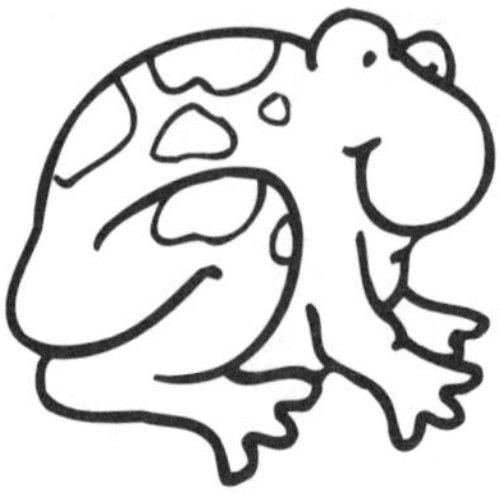

frog

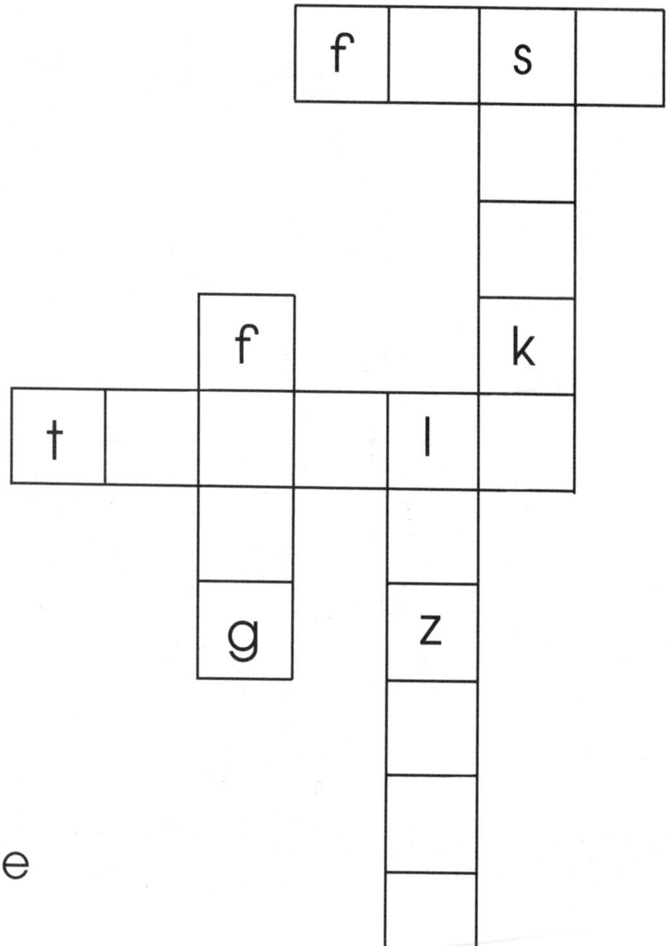

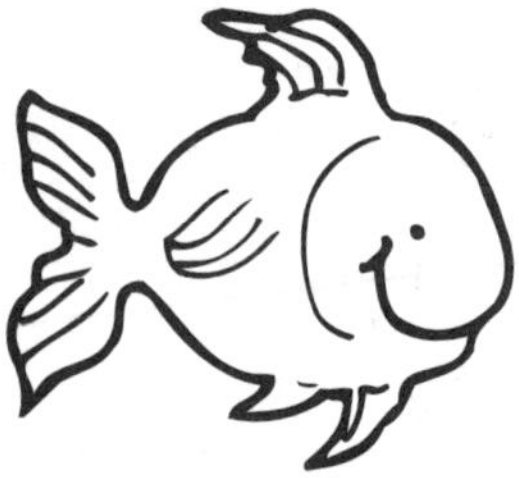

fish

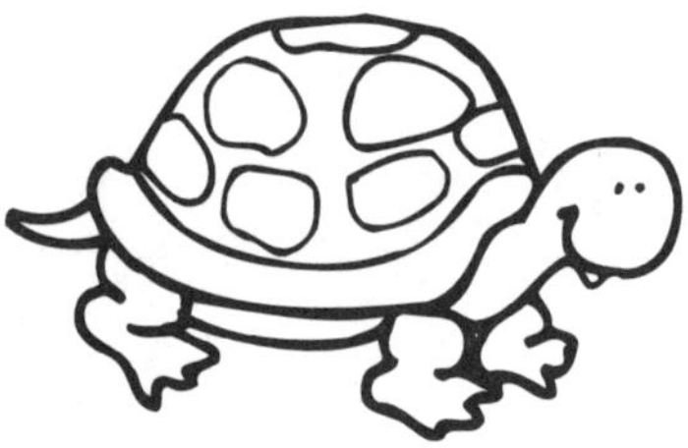

turtle

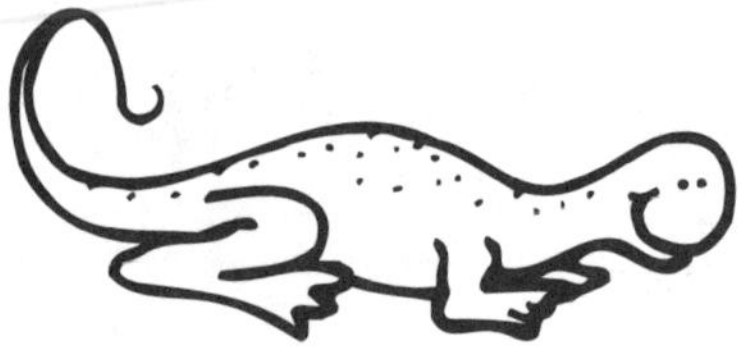

lizard

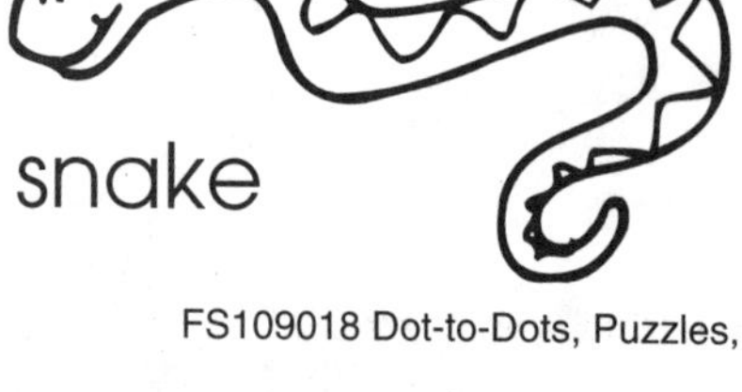

snake

Name _____

Sweet and Cool

Connect the dots from **A** to **Z**. Color.

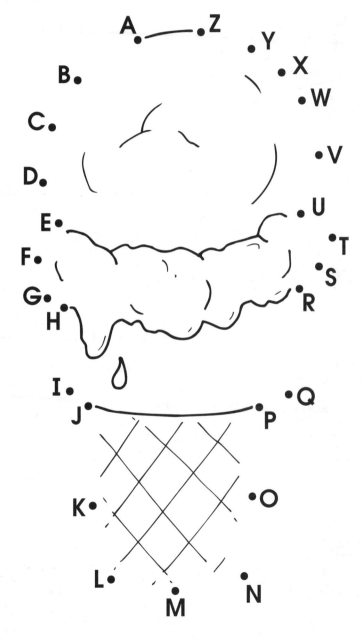

Great job,

_____!

You worked hard completing lots of dot-to-dots, puzzles, and games!

_____
signature

_____
date